The Visual Guide to

Asperger's Syndrome and Puberty

D1620632

by Alis Rowe

Also by Alis Rowe

One Lonely Mind
978-0-9562693-0-0

The Girl with the Curly Hair - Asperger's and Me
978-0-9562693-2-4

The 1st Comic Book
978-0-9562693-1-7

The 2nd Comic Book
978-0-9562693-4-8

The 3rd Comic Book
978-0-9562693-3-1

The 4th Comic Book
978-15086839-7-1

Websites:
www.alisrowe.co.uk
www.thegirlwiththecurlyhair.co.uk
www.womensweightlifting.co.uk

Social Media:
www.facebook.com/thegirlwiththecurlyhair
www.twitter.com/curlyhairedalis

The Visual Guide to

Asperger's Syndrome and Puberty

by Alis Rowe

Lonely Mind Books
London

For girls with ASD and their parents

hello

Puberty is a difficult time for everyone and probably even more so for children on the spectrum. When you take into account that a person with ASD (Autism Spectrum Disorder) typically already has hypersensitivities, anxiety and mood swings, as well as problems communicating, it is easy to see why puberty is going to be so hard for them.

As well as all these physical and emotional changes, puberty tends to happen at a time of big transition, i.e. when children are moving from primary to secondary school. All of these things can cause an increase in anxiety.

I hope this book provides some insight and strategies on dealing with puberty and how parents and children can make things a bit easier.

Alis aka The Girl with the Curly Hair

Contents

PUBERTY CREATES CHALLENGES FOR ALL CHILDREN, HOWEVER CHILDREN WITH ASD MAY HAVE MORE, OR DIFFERENT, CHALLENGES DURING THIS TIME

A GIRL WITH ASD MAY KEEP UP INTELLECTUALLY WITH HER PEERS (OR EVEN BE AHEAD), BUT LAG BEHIND SOCIALLY AND EMOTIONALLY, E.G.:

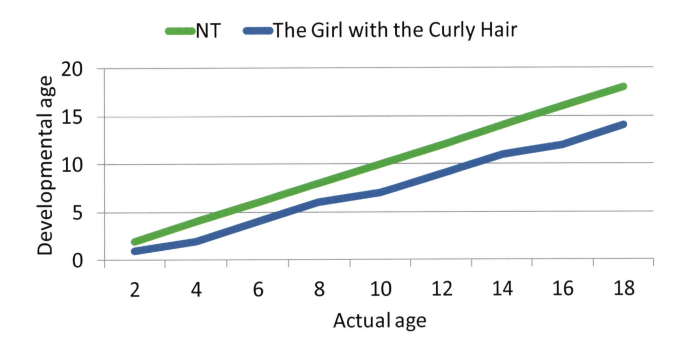

THIS MEANS THAT A GIRL WITH ASD WILL OFTEN FEEL YOUNGER – AND BEHAVE YOUNGER – THAN HER AGE IN SOCIAL SITUATIONS

THIS MAKES LIFE VERY HARD BECAUSE, AT SCHOOL, THE GIRL WITH ASD IS SURROUNDED BY NTS WHO BEHAVE VERY DIFFERENTLY

TEENAGE NTS ARE LIKELY TO...

- SHOW MORE CONCERN ABOUT APPEARANCE
- BE INFLUENCED BY THEIR PEERS

TEENAGE NTS CAN USUALLY...

- EXPRESS FEELINGS THROUGH TALKING
- CONSTRUCT HYPOTHETICAL SOLUTIONS TO PROBLEMS
- DISTINGUISH FACT FROM OPINION

TEENAGE NTS CAN, OR WANT, TO...

- CHOOSE THEIR OWN CLOTHES
- KEEP UP WITH PERSONAL HYGIENE – THEY KNOW WHEN TO BRUSH THEIR TEETH, SHOWER, WASH CLOTHES, ETC.
- MAKE THEIR OWN FOOD
- GO OUT OF THE HOUSE ON THEIR OWN

SHE WILL HAVE SOME DIFFICULTIES WITH THESE THINGS. SHE FEELS DIFFERENT BECAUSE SHE IS DIFFERENT

BECAUSE THESE MILESTONES WERE NOT MET UNTIL MUCH LATER, THERE WERE SOCIAL AND EMOTIONAL CONSEQUENCES FOR THE GIRL WITH THE CURLY HAIR:

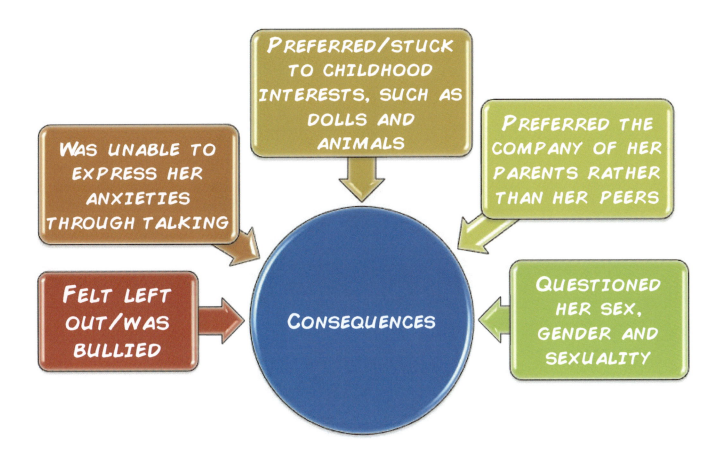

PREFERRED/STUCK TO CHILDHOOD INTERESTS, SUCH AS DOLLS AND ANIMALS

WAS UNABLE TO EXPRESS HER ANXIETIES THROUGH TALKING

PREFERRED THE COMPANY OF HER PARENTS RATHER THAN HER PEERS

FELT LEFT OUT/WAS BULLIED

CONSEQUENCES

QUESTIONED HER SEX, GENDER AND SEXUALITY

SHE FELT LEFT OUT, DIFFERENT, ABNORMAL AND INFERIOR

LET'S LOOK AT THESE
PROBLEMS AND THINK
ABOUT POSSIBLE
SOLUTIONS FOR THEM

Problem: Felt left out/was bullied

- After puberty, PEERS were less willing to tolerate someone who was different
- The Girl with the Curly Hair still couldn't tie her shoelaces or ride a bike. She also still needed her parents to choose her clothes and make meals for her
- During a time in life when everyone else was interested in fashion and fads, she preferred to dress in the same comfortable outfit everyday
- She was philosophical and contemplated, for example, the meaning of life, which did not appear to cross the minds of others
- Whereas when she was younger she did have some friends, the older they all got the more distant they became
- She felt really anxious interacting with her peers because she didn't understand some of the things they said and couldn't relate to their interests

Solutions

- Socialising with people over the internet provided a source of companionship - there was no need to understand body language and the socialising could take place in the safe, quiet environment of home, at times that suited her
- Spending time with older people and younger people made her feel much less anxious than time spent with people her own age due to reduced peer pressure
- Finding one good friend was her lifeline

PROBLEM: WAS UNABLE TO EXPRESS FEELINGS THROUGH TALKING

REASONS

- **ASD** IS A COMMUNICATION DISORDER – TRANSLATING THOUGHTS AND FEELINGS INTO WORDS IS REALLY DIFFICULT
- THE GIRL WITH THE CURLY HAIR COULD NOT EVEN MAKE SENSE OF HER OWN THOUGHTS AND FEELINGS
- SHE FELT THAT NO ONE WOULD UNDERSTAND HER ANYWAY

SOLUTIONS

- KEEPING A DIARY WAS USEFUL IN RECORDING DAILY EVENTS AND SEEING TRENDS IN FEELINGS/THOUGHTS BASED ON WHAT WAS HAPPENING EACH DAY
- COMMUNICATING WITH FAMILY AND FRIENDS IN WRITING (E.G. TEXT MESSAGE, EMAIL, SOCIAL MEDIA) WAS LESS ANXIETY-PROVOKING, LESS CONFUSING, AND GENERALLY EASIER AND MORE FUN!

Problem: Preferred childhood interests

Reasons

- She was emotionally and socially less mature than her peers
- She didn't have any friends so created her own imaginary ones to fill the void
- She used dolls to learn social rules, so the way she played mimicked the people and characters she came across in real life
- She enjoyed being on her own with toys and games or dolls and soft/plastic animals – things that didn't have to involve other people

Solutions

- Parents supporting her solitary play was important as it made her feel validated
- Parents structuring activities with other children, such baking cakes, bike rides, bowling, etc.
- It might have been helpful if she'd had younger children to play with or to mentor

Problem: Preferred the company of her parents over PEERS

Reasons

- Parents were familiar, steady and predictable, whereas PEERS were fast paced, changing and confusing
- She understood the social rules at home but not in her PEER GROUP
- She felt she could be herself at home with family, whereas at school she was bullied and mocked
- There was an enormous amount of trust in her parents that, if she had a meltdown, they would help her and not taunt her
- At home, things were 'normal' so she felt normal. At school, things and people were different and changing, so she felt isolated
- The Girl with the Curly Hair had sophisticated and formal vocabulary for her age that her PEERS did not understand

Solutions

- Parents can help by writing the meaning of colloquial teenage expressions on a board or the fridge
- Interacting with adults is still developing social skills
- Role play with an adult who is pretending to be a teenager can help practice what to say and do

Problem: Questioned her sex/gender/sexuality

Reasons

- She did not fit in with her PEERS
- She did not relate to people her own age
- She did not understand romantic relationships
- She did not relate to society's presentation of 'being female'
- She did not like maintaining personal hygiene, let alone removing body hair
- She did not like wearing a bra

Solutions

- Parents can encourage reading or watching material which illustrate diversity
- Parents talking about it being OK to wear whatever she likes – it's OK for girls to wear "boy clothes" and boys to wear "girl clothes"
- Parents allowing her to develop her own identity without pressurising her to conform to societal norms

At this age, the 'Glass Jar' feeling is very strong

WHEN SOCIALISING WITH OTHER GIRLS, THE GIRL WITH THE CURLY HAIR ENDED UP FEELING VERY ANXIOUS AND VERY LOW...

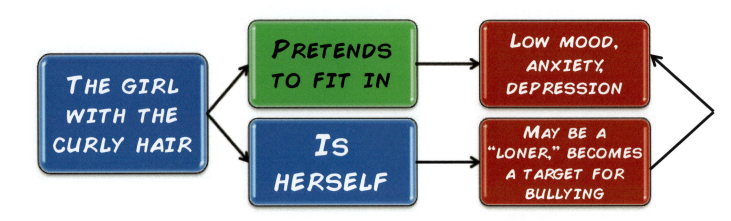

SOME GIRLS WITH ASD WILL FLICK BETWEEN THE TWO, OTHERS WILL BEHAVE LIKE ONE OR THE OTHER

SHE FOUND COMPANIONSHIP IN BOYS...

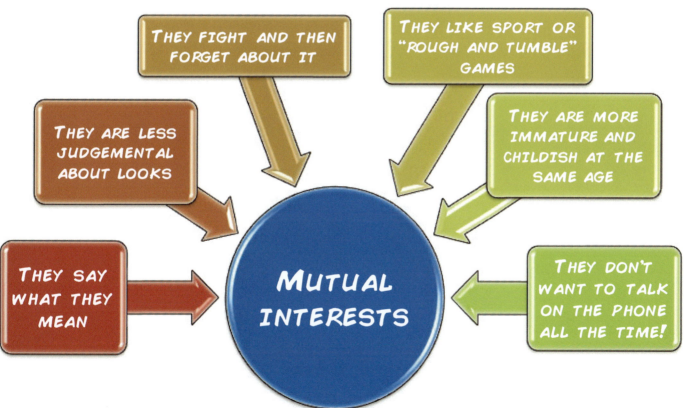

THEY FIGHT AND THEN FORGET ABOUT IT

THEY LIKE SPORT OR "ROUGH AND TUMBLE" GAMES

THEY ARE LESS JUDGEMENTAL ABOUT LOOKS

THEY ARE MORE IMMATURE AND CHILDISH AT THE SAME AGE

THEY SAY WHAT THEY MEAN

MUTUAL INTERESTS

THEY DON'T WANT TO TALK ON THE PHONE ALL THE TIME!

...WHICH IS LOVELY, BUT IT IS VERY IMPORTANT GIRLS UNDERSTAND THAT, JUST LIKE GIRLS CHANGE DURING PUBERTY, SO WILL BOYS

EVEN IF IT'S A COUPLE OF YEARS LATER

WHEN *THE GIRL WITH THE CURLY HAIR* WAS AT SCHOOL, BOYS AND GIRLS WERE SEPARATED FOR 'SEX EDUCATION' LESSONS

DUE TO IMPAIRED SOCIAL IMAGINATION, SHE COULD NOT IMAGINE WHAT THE BOYS WERE TAUGHT WHEN THEY WENT AWAY. IN FACT, IT NEVER EVEN OCCURRED TO HER THAT THEY WERE GOING THROUGH PUBERTY TOO

What does The Girl with the Curly Hair think is especially important to know about boys and puberty?

Change in boy friend	Consequence for female friend
He might start caring more about his appearance, e.g. wearing different, "trendy" clothes and changing his hairstyle	May feel anxious that her boy friend looks like a 'different' person
He might become more interested in girls and dating	May feel lonely that her boy friend is less interested in playing video games with her
He might start flirting with her and want to hug more often	May think he is just being nice/cannot see any hidden agenda
He might start caring more about what other boys and girls think of him	May feel lonely and upset that he no longer wants to spend as much time with her/be seen to be hanging out with her
His interests may change from video games and football, to girls, fashion and music	May feel isolated and disconnected, that she is being left behind whilst everyone else around her appears to be changing

The Girl with the Curly Hair

Found her own physical changes very hard to cope with, e.g.

Noticing that her body was changing or noticing that other girls' bodies were changing was very scary

The hardest thing was still feeling like a young girl, yet she was beginning to look like an adult

She did not like to look at herself naked because she said "That is not me"

Favourite clothes started to become too small

THERE WERE SOME GOOD THINGS ABOUT BECOMING AN ADULT HOWEVER...

BEING ABLE TO DRIVE

BEING ABLE TO VOTE

GOING OUT OF THE HOUSE ON YOUR OWN

EARNING MONEY

...AND SHE FOUND IT HELPFUL WHEN HER PARENTS REMINDED HER OF THESE THINGS

PHYSICAL CHANGES DURING PUBERTY:

HER HIPS MAY GET WIDER

SHE MIGHT PUT ON WEIGHT

SHE DEVELOPS BREASTS

SHE HAS HER FIRST PERIOD

SHE GETS TALLER

THESE PHYSICAL CHANGES CAUSED ENORMOUS AMOUNTS OF ANXIETY

SOCIAL CHANGES DURING PUBERTY:

SHE BECOMES VERY AWARE OF HERSELF (DEVELOPMENT OF 'EGO')	SHE BECOMES VERY AWARE OF OTHERS

THIS MEANT THAT SHE STARTED TO RECOGNISE THE GENDER AND SEXUAL ORIENTATION OF HERSELF – AND OTHER PEOPLE

THE GIRL WITH THE CURLY HAIR THINKS IT IS IMPORTANT FOR GIRLS WITH ASD AND THEIR PARENTS TO DISCUSS A FEW THINGS...

HOW DID YOU GET TO BECOME MALE OR FEMALE?

WHY IS THE POPULATION OF THE WORLD ROUGHLY HALF AND HALF?

WHY ARE SOME BABIES GIRLS AND SOME BABIES BOYS?

HOW WOULD YOU FEEL IF YOU WOKE UP TOMORROW AS A BOY INSTEAD?

The Girl with the Curly Hair

talked with her parents about why they are together

THE GIRL WITH THE CURLY HAIR THOUGHT THIS WAS INTERESTING. SHE THOUGHT THEY WERE TOGETHER BECAUSE...

GENDER IDENTITY

THE GIRL WITH THE CURLY HAIR STRUGGLED TO IDENTIFY HERSELF AS 'FEMALE'

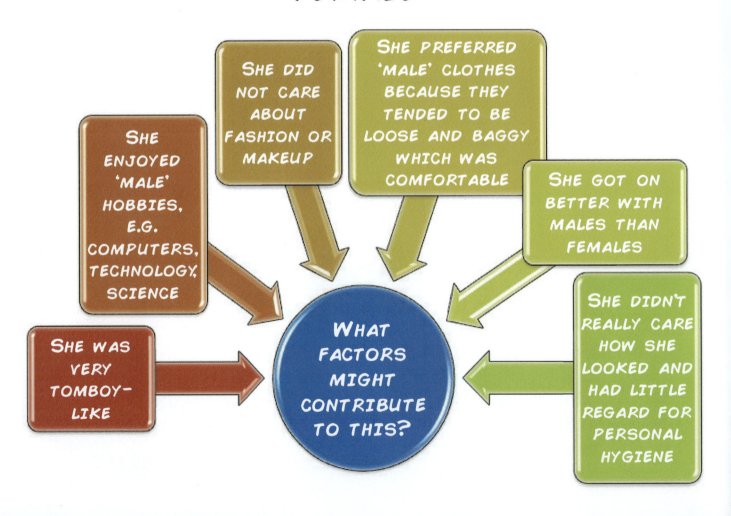

SEXUALITY

THE GENERAL IDEA IS SEXUALITY CAN BE EXPRESSED IN A VARIETY OF WAYS, E.G.

LESS COMMON
ASEXUAL: NOT BEING SEXUALLY ATTRACTED
TO ANYONE

MORE COMMON
HOMOSEXUAL (GAY/LESBIAN): BEING
SEXUALLY ATTRACTED TO THE SAME SEX

MORE COMMON
BISEXUAL: BEING SEXUALLY ATTRACTED TO
PEOPLE OF BOTH SEXES

MOST COMMON
HETEROSEXUAL: BEING SEXUALLY ATTRACTED
TO PEOPLE OF THE OPPOSITE SEX

IT IS PERFECTLY **OK** TO BE ANY OF THEM!

THE GIRL WITH THE CURLY HAIR THINKS A HIGH PROPORTION OF PEOPLE WITH ASD STRUGGLE TO DEFINE THEIR SEXUALITY

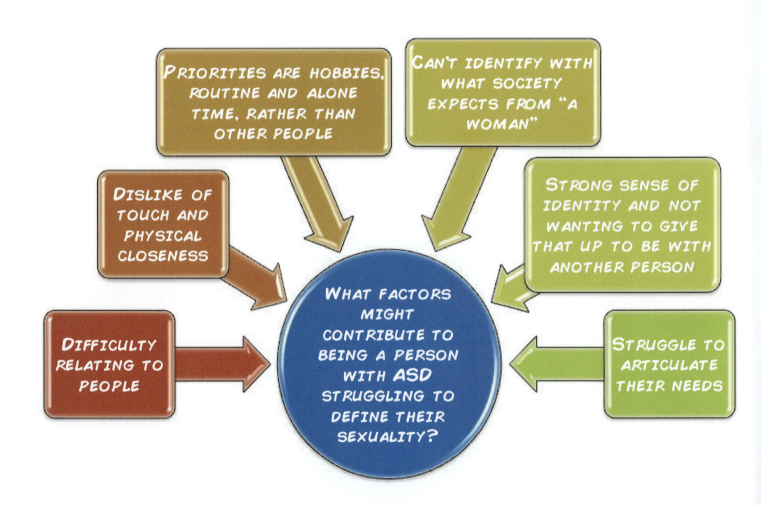

THE GIRL WITH THE CURLY HAIR THINKS THAT MANY **PEOPLE WITH ASD** MAY BE ASEXUAL

SHE THINKS THAT MANY MAY BE BISEXUAL OR PREFER TO SEE THE PERSON FOR THEIR PERSONALITY RATHER THAN THEIR SEX

PERIODS

ADVICE FOR PARENTS AND THEIR DAUGHTERS

The Girl with the Curly Hair needed to understand the biology of having periods because **People with ASD** need to know the 'why' more than other people!

Parents ought to explain very clearly exactly what happens using the correct anatomical terms. Use diagrams if necessary

When preparing for her first period, it may be helpful to:

Put red food colouring in her

UNDERWEAR TO SHOW WHAT BLOOD MIGHT LOOK LIKE WHEN SHE STARTS HER PERIOD

SHOW HER HOW TO PUT A SANITARY TOWEL ON (CREATE A SEQUENCE OF VISUALS AND STICK THEM ON THE WALL)

MARK THE KNICKERS WITH WHERE THE SANITARY TOWEL SHOULD BE PLACED

MAKE SURE SHE REALISES TO WEAR THEM AT NIGHT

HERE ARE SOME QUESTIONS ABOUT PERIODS THAT THE GIRL WITH THE CURLY HAIR HAD

"How do I know when my period is due?"

You can keep a calendar and mark the start and end days of your period, as well as the days in between, e.g.:

Over time, you will be able to work out average length of period and due date (there are some good apps that can do this automatically)

Be aware that periods are not always the same length or same frequency, especially in the first few years

You may have one **28** days after the last, then the next one **32** days, the next one **30**, etc. ... some months you may miss a period completely

It is helpful to chart them anyway, just in case there is a trend. As the months and years go on, you will find they are easier to predict

If you have any worries and need to see a GP, it will be helpful to have your chart for them to look at

You may also notice some physical signs that your period is due, e.g.:

Your breasts, stomach and lower back may feel sore or achy
You may get one or two extra spots on your face

You may also notice some emotional signs that your period is due, e.g.:

You may feel more upset about things, more emotional, angry, sad, frustrated... or other emotions

Around the time your period is due, it is helpful to carry a sanitary towel or tampon in your bag, just in case your period starts when you are not at home

If you forget, don't panic, periods usually start very light and a little bit of blood on your underwear won't be visible to anyone else

You can put a bit of tissue in your underwear temporarily

There are machines in some public toilets where you can buy sanitary towels and tampons

"HOW DO I DEAL WITH THE PAIN?"

Hot water bottle on your stomach

Hot water bottle on your lower back

Painkillers (check with your parents or GP)

A hot bath (bleeding stops when you're in the bath so don't worry. Also, hygiene is extra important at this time)

MAKE SURE YOU ARE AWARE THAT TO HAVE STOMACH AND LOWER BACK PAIN IS VERY NORMAL DURING YOUR PERIOD (SOME GIRLS DON'T REALISE THIS AND MAY WORRY THAT NORMAL PERIOD PAIN IS ACTUALLY APPENDICITIS!)

"How do I know when to change a sanitary towel?"

It is a personal decision...

The Girl with the Curly Hair changes hers every 4 hours

Unless it is very heavy and she can see it is completely covered in blood... in which case she will change it then

Most 'night' sanitary towels can be left in overnight so you will not need to wake up during the night to change it

IT MAY BE HELPFUL FOR YOU TO GET INTO A ROUTINE OF WHEN TO CHANGE IT BASED ON YOUR SCHOOL SCHEDULE, E.G. ...

TIME	SCHEDULE
8.45AM	REGISTRATION
9AM	LESSON 1
10AM	LESSON 2
11AM	BREAK*
11.15AM	LESSON 3
12.15PM	LUNCH
1PM	LESSON 4
2PM	LESSON 5
3PM	HOME TIME*

*TIME TO CHANGE SANITARY TOWEL/TAMPON

CONSIDER KEEPING THE TIMES THE SAME WHEN YOU ARE AT HOME TOO. THE CONSISTENCY MAY MAKE IT EASIER TO REMEMBER

"WHERE DO I PUT USED SANITARY TOWELS?"

PUBLIC TOILETS SHOULD HAVE A SPECIAL DISPOSAL UNIT*

IF YOU ARE EMBARRASSED AT SCHOOL, PUT THEM IN A PLASTIC BAG AND BRING THEM HOME AND DISPOSE OF THEM AT HOME

AT HOME, THROW THEM AWAY WITH THE RUBBISH*

*THE GIRL WITH THE CURLY HAIR DOES NOT LIKE THE WORD B.I.N. SO TRIES TO AVOID USING IT WHEREVER POSSIBLE!!!

"HOW DO I TELL PEOPLE THAT I AM EXPERIENCING PERIOD PAIN?"

YOU CAN BE COMPLETELY OPEN AND SAY, "I HAVE PERIOD PAIN"

YOU CAN COME UP WITH A PARTICULAR SIGN, FOR EXAMPLE, YOU AND YOUR PARENTS MAY AGREE THAT WHEN YOU POINT TO YOUR STOMACH, IT MEANS YOU'VE GOT PERIOD PAIN

YOU CAN BE MORE SUBTLE AND SAY "I HAVE STOMACH/BACK ACHE" (SOME PEOPLE WILL AUTOMATICALLY KNOW WHAT YOU ARE TRYING TO SAY IF YOU SAY THIS)

IF ANY OF THOSE ARE TOO HARD, YOU CAN JUST SAY "I AM NOT FEELING WELL"

FEELINGS

Mood swings are very common during and after puberty

It is a good idea to understand how you are feeling so that 1) you can communicate it to others and 2) you know how to uplift yourself

A BASIC NUMBER SCALE CAN BE USED TO IDENTIFY HOW YOU ARE FEELING, E.G.

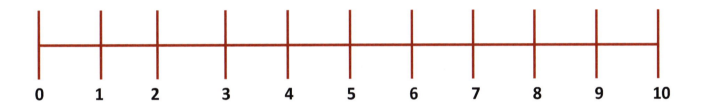

0 1 2 3 4 5 6 7 8 9 10

0=VERY HAPPY/RELAXED
10=VERY UNHAPPY/ANXIOUS

THERMOMETER SCALES CAN BE USED FOR ANGER AND SADNESS:

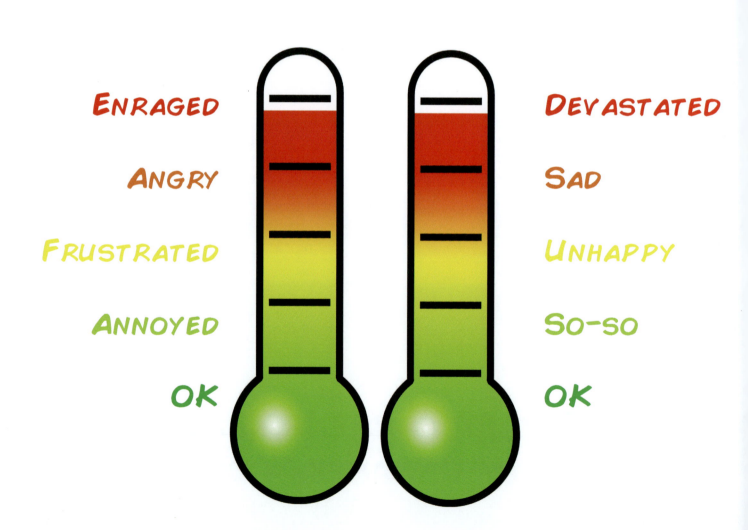

The Girl with the Curly Hair

FOUND IT DIFFICULT TO KNOW WHAT THE DIFFERENT FEELINGS FELT LIKE, SO SHE MADE A SCRAPBOOK OF THE DIFFERENT SORTS OF SITUATIONS WHICH MADE HER FEEL EACH WAY, E.G.

Feeling	Situation
Devastated	When her cat died
Sad	When her cat was unwell
Unhappy	When she got some questions wrong in her homework assignment; when there were no more socks – of the particular colour she wanted – left in the shop; when she got something she did not want at Christmas
So-so	When she got a present she didn't ask for at Christmas; when she had to wear another pair of trousers because the other ones weren't clean
OK	When her cat was well; when she got lots of questions right in her homework assignment; when she got the socks she wanted; when she was able to wear the pair of trousers she wanted

She found it helpful to make a list of all the things she could do when she was feeling somewhere between, say, 5 and 10 on the number scale, or yellow and red on the thermometer scale, that would make her feel better, e.g.:

The Girl with the Curly Hair likes to...

- Take her dog for a walk
- Stroke or brush her cats
- Jump on her trampoline
- Go on the swing
- Read a book
- Play a computer game
- Have a bath
- Take a nap

Parents can make sure their DAUGHTER has a safe place she can go to when she has emotional outbursts. The obvious place is her bedroom but if she shares a room with a sibling, another more private space may need to be found, e.g. a tent!

Children with ASD may find sensory equipment soothing, e.g. weighted blankets, lava lamps, bubble tubes...

HYGIENE

SOME CHILDREN WITH ASD DO NOT EVEN NOTICE THEY NEED TO WASH. OTHERS ARE RELUCTANT TO TAKE CARE OF THEIR PERSONAL HYGIENE

THIS IS USUALLY TO DO WITH ANXIETY...

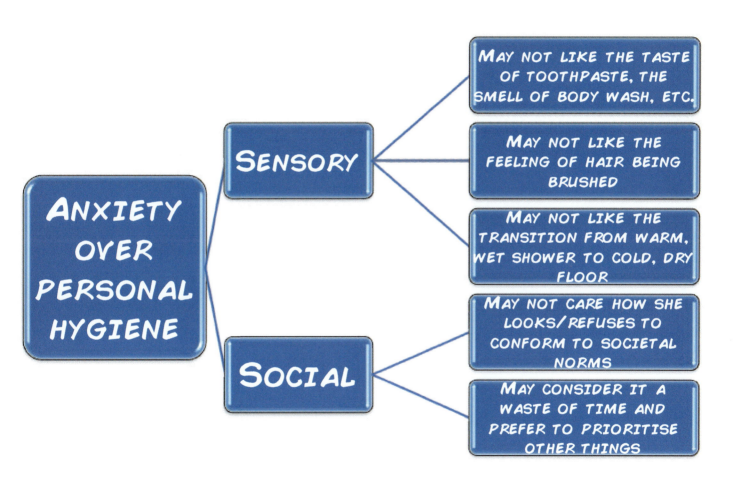

ANXIETY OVER PERSONAL HYGIENE

SENSORY

- MAY NOT LIKE THE TASTE OF TOOTHPASTE, THE SMELL OF BODY WASH, ETC.
- MAY NOT LIKE THE FEELING OF HAIR BEING BRUSHED
- MAY NOT LIKE THE TRANSITION FROM WARM, WET SHOWER TO COLD, DRY FLOOR

SOCIAL

- MAY NOT CARE HOW SHE LOOKS/REFUSES TO CONFORM TO SOCIETAL NORMS
- MAY CONSIDER IT A WASTE OF TIME AND PREFER TO PRIORITISE OTHER THINGS

69

Tips for parents to help their DAUGHTER with personal hygiene

FIND TOILETRIES THEY CAN TOLERATE

- CHILDREN'S TOOTHPASTES OR MILD MINT MAY BE MORE COMFORTABLE THAN STRONG MINT

- UNSCENTED ROLL ON DEODORANTS OR NATURAL CRYSTAL ANTIPERSPIRANTS

- AN ELECTRIC TOOTHBRUSH MAY BE BETTER THAN A MANUAL ONE – THE CONSISTENT MOVEMENT IS PREDICTABLE

- 2 IN 1 HAIR WASH CAN SAVE TIME

Establish a Routine

- Incorporate bath time into the daily routine so that she always knows exactly when it is happening and that it is going to happen

- Schedule an enjoyable task after the bath or shower (reward)

- Use a visual timetable on the bedroom wall

CREATE A BETTER BATH/SHOWER ENVIRONMENT

- INCORPORATE THEIR SPECIAL INTEREST, E.G. TOY FISH COULD GO IN THE BATH WITH THEM

- GOGGLES CAN BE USED WHEN WASHING HAIR OR FACE

- USE A SECURE BATH MAT

- HAVE THE DRESSING GOWN READY IMMEDIATELY OR A WARM TOWEL TO MAKE THE TRANSITION FROM HOT TO COLD/WET TO DRY LESS OF A SHOCK

- USE FUN TIMERS SO THEY KNOW EXACTLY HOW LONG THEY'VE GOT LEFT TO BRUSH TEETH/SHOWER

Talk about societal expectations and the reasons for good personal hygiene

- If they don't look/smell pleasant, people won't want to be around them

- Poor personal hygiene can lead to being bullied

- They don't have to look like other TEENAGE GIRLS but it is important to be clean

REMIND OF SENSORY CONSEQUENCES THAT NEGATIVELY AFFECT THEM

- THEY MIGHT HATE HOW THEIR HAIR FEELS WHEN IT'S GREASY

- THEY MIGHT FIND IT DIFFICULT TO SLEEP IF THEIR TOENAILS ARE LONG

- THEY MIGHT FIND IT DIFFICULT TO WRITE/TYPE/DRAW (OR DO OTHER HOBBIES) IF THEIR FINGERNAILS ARE LONG

- THEY MIGHT HATE COMBING THEIR HAIR BUT, THE MORE OFTEN THEY WASH IT, THE EASIER THE COMBING IS

- THEY MIGHT HATE THE FEELING OF SWEAT ON THEIR BODY

DATING

THE GIRL WITH THE CURLY HAIR WAS VERY INNOCENT AND NAIVE, E.G. ...

SHE COULD NOT TELL WHEN SOMEONE WAS MAKING A JOKE OR BEING SARCASTIC, OR WHEN THEY WERE TEASING

SHE USED TO BUY HER FRIEND A BIRTHDAY GIFT, DESPITE THE FACT HER FRIEND NEVER ONCE EVEN REMEMBERED HERS

HER BELIEFS COULD BE EASILY SWAYED IF SOMEONE WAS BETTER OR MORE CONFIDENT AT ASSERTING THEIR OPINION

SHE BELIEVED SHE WAS PRETTY WHEN BOYS TOLD HER. SHE THOUGHT THEY WERE BEING HONEST AND NICE

SHE WOULD GIVE MONEY TO FRIENDS IF THEY ASKED TO BORROW IT, EVEN IF THEY NEVER PAID IT BACK

SHE COULD NOT BELIEVE THAT SOMEONE WHO WAS BEING NICE TO HER FACE MIGHT HAVE BEEN BEING CRUEL BEHIND HER BACK

SHE BELIEVED THAT WHEN PEOPLE CRIED, THEY TRULY WERE SAD AND COULD NOT UNDERSTAND 'CROCODILE TEARS'

SHE WALKED HER NEIGHBOUR'S DOG SEVERAL TIMES A WEEK, BUT NEVER REALLY GOT ANY THANKS

GIRLS WITH ASD DO TEND TO BE MORE VULNERABLE THAN THEIR NT PEERS

PARENTS REALLY NEED TO LOOK AFTER THEIR LITTLE GIRLS AND THE FIRST STEP IS EDUCATING THEM

At a time when OTHER GIRLS started dating boys, The Girl with the Curly Hair could not relate to it...

She felt too young and was not interested (remember that ASD is a developmental disability so sexual behaviours and interest may come later than you expect)

Some GIRLS WITH ASD will pretend to be interested in dating, in order to 'FIT IN'... but this can be dangerous

THE PRIVATE PARTS RULES*

PARENTS CAN TEACH THEIR DAUGHTER THE FOLLOWING THINGS OR YOU CAN FOLLOW IT YOURSELF TO HELP UNDERSTAND WHEN TOUCHING IS OR IS NOT APPROPRIATE

IF IT HAS TO DO WITH PRIVATE PARTS

IT HAS TO BE DONE IN A PRIVATE PLACE AT A PRIVATE TIME

IF IT INVOLVES SOMEONE ELSE THEN YOU NEED TO HAVE THEIR PERMISSION

*Lynne Moxon, Issues within Puberty & Sexuality in people with Autism Spectrum Disorders, PowerPoint presentation, ESPA, Northumbria University.

Peer Pressure

Just because...	It doesn't mean...
OTHER GIRLS ARE SPENDING THEIR FREE TIME WITH BOYS	YOU HAVE TO. DO YOU WANT TO? IF YOU DON'T, DON'T!
OTHER GIRLS AND BOYS HAVE STARTED KISSING AND HOLDING HANDS WITH ONE ANOTHER	YOU HAVE TO. IT IS WRONG TO KISS AND TOUCH OTHER PEOPLE WITHOUT THEIR PERMISSION. IF YOU DON'T WANT TO DO IT, YOU HAVE A RIGHT TO SAY "NO"
OTHER GIRLS TALK ABOUT CERTAIN BOYS BEING "HOT" OR "GOOD LOOKING"	YOU HAVE TO THINK THE SAME. SOMEONE WHO IS "GOOD LOOKING" TO ONE PERSON MAY BE UNATTRACTIVE TO SOMEONE ELSE. IT'S VERY INDIVIDUAL
OTHER YOUNG PEOPLE ARE SAYING THAT THEY'VE "HAD SEX"	THAT THEY ARE ACTUALLY DOING IT (PEOPLE LIE)

GOING OUT SAFELY

TRY TO ALWAYS GO OUT WITH ANOTHER PERSON, SUCH AS MUM, DAD OR A FRIEND

IF YOU GO OUT ON YOUR OWN, MAKE SURE YOU KNOW WHERE YOU ARE GOING BEFORE YOU SET OFF AND ALWAYS TAKE YOUR MOBILE PHONE

A BAG THAT GOES ROUND YOUR BODY OR ON YOUR BACK IS SAFER THAN ONE YOU CARRY IN YOUR HAND

KEEP YOUR BAG WITH YOU AT ALL TIMES (WHEN SITTING DOWN, WRAP THE STRAP OF THE BAG AROUND THE CHAIR OR TABLE LEG)

DO NOT CARRY ALL YOUR IMPORTANT THINGS IN THIS ONE BAG (KEEP SOME STUFF AT HOME OR IN YOUR POCKETS)

NO MATTER HOW MUCH YOU WANT TO BE ON YOUR OWN, IT'S SAFEST TO STAY WITH OTHER PEOPLE, SO ALWAYS SIT IN A CARRIAGE IN THE TRAIN THAT HAS PEOPLE ON IT, AND WALK DOWN THE MAIN ROAD, NOT THE ALLEY WAY

To finish off, *The Girl with the Curly Hair* wants GIRLS and their parents to understand that...

A GIRL WITH ASD IS PROBABLY GOING TO BE EMOTIONALLY YOUNGER THAN HER NT PEERS (THINK ABOUT THE EFFECT THIS IS GOING TO HAVE ON HER AND THE WAY SHE BUILDS RELATIONSHIPS)

NT TEENAGERS OFTEN STRUGGLE WITH THEIR SEXUALITY. THINK ABOUT HOW MUCH MORE CONFUSING IT IS LIKELY TO BE FOR A GIRL WITH ASD, WHO DOESN'T FIT IN, HAS VERY FEW — IF ANY — FRIENDS, AND GENERALLY FEELS SHE DOESN'T REALLY RELATE TO ANYONE

GIRLS WITH ASD TEND TO BE INNOCENT AND NAIVE AND CONSEQUENTLY THEY ARE VULNERABLE. BE PROACTIVE ABOUT SEX EDUCATION, AND TALK ABOUT RELATIONSHIPS AND STAYING SAFE

Hints for a good sex education programme. Consider including:

Bodies – male and female, naming of body parts, function of body parts

Puberty

Periods

Hygiene

Sexual activity, including why people have sex, appropriate places to have sex, good and bad touching, pressures to have sex, who makes decisions about sex, reasons for saying "no", role playing saying "no", preventing abuse and what to do if it happens

Many thanks for reading

Other books in The Visual Guides series at the time of writing:

The Visual Guide to Asperger's Syndrome

The Visual Guide to Asperger's Syndrome: Meltdowns and Shutdowns

The Visual Guide to Asperger's Syndrome in 5-8 Year Olds

The Visual Guide to Asperger's Syndrome in 8-11 Year Olds

The Visual Guide to Asperger's Syndrome in 13-16 Year Olds

The Visual Guide to Asperger's Syndrome in 16-18 Year Olds

The Visual Guide to Asperger's Syndrome for the Neurotypical Partner

The Visual Guide to Asperger's Syndrome: Social Energy

The Visual Guide to Asperger's Syndrome and Anxiety

The Visual Guide to Asperger's Syndrome: Helping Siblings

New titles are continually being produced so keep an eye out!

Printed in Poland
by Amazon Fulfillment
Poland Sp. z o.o., Wrocław